First Facts

The Solar System

Space Shuttles

by Steve Kortenkamp

Consultant:
James Gerard
Aerospace Education Specialist, NASA
Kennedy Space Center, Florida

Capstone
press

Mankato, Minnesota

First Facts is published by Capstone Press,
151 Good Counsel Drive, P.O. Box 669, Mankato, Minnesota 56002.
www.capstonepress.com

Library of Congress Cataloging-in-Publication Data
Kortenkamp, Steve.
    Space shuttles / by Steve Kortenkamp.
        p. cm. — (First facts. The solar system)
    Summary: "Describes the history and uses of NASA's space shuttles" — Provided
by publisher.
    Includes bibliographical references and index.
    ISBN–13: 978–1–4296–1259–3 (hardcover)
    ISBN–10: 1–4296–1259–2 (hardcover)
    1. Space shuttles — United States — Juvenile literature. I. Title. II. Series.
TL795.515.K67 2008
629.44'1 — dc22   2007023028

Editorial Credits
Lori Shores and Christopher L. Harbo, editors; Juliette Peters, set designer; Kim Brown,
    book designer; Linda Clavel, photo researcher

Photo Credits
Corbis/Roger Ressmeyer/NASA, 10
NASA, 1, 5, 6, 9, 12, 13, 14, 15, 16 (both), 17 (both), 19, 20, 21, cover
Photodisc, back cover
Photo Researchers Inc./SPL, 8

1 2 3 4 5 6 13 12 11 10 09 08

Table of Contents

The First Reusable Spacecraft

Until 1981, NASA used a new spacecraft for every space trip. Then the United States began using the world's first reusable spacecraft. It's called the space shuttle. A space shuttle carries equipment and astronauts to space and then back to Earth.

5

external tank

solid rocket boosters

main engines

Atlantis

NASA

6

Up Like a Rocket

To launch, a space shuttle uses two solid rocket **boosters** and three main engines. The solid rocket boosters lift a shuttle off the launch pad and high into the sky. Then the main engines push the shuttle into **orbit**. A giant **external tank** carries fuel for the shuttle's main engines.

Fun Fact!
The solid rocket boosters separate from the external tank. Parachutes carry them back to Earth. The rocket boosters are reused for the next shuttle launch.

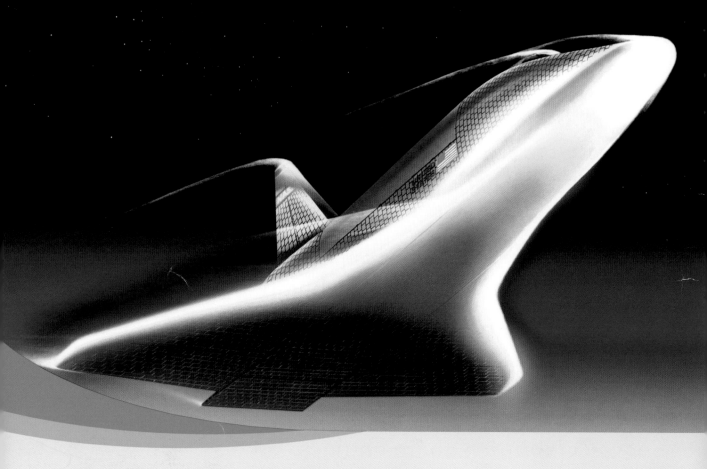

Down Like an Airplane

The space shuttle launches like a rocket. But it lands more like an airplane. The air slows down the shuttle as it reenters Earth's atmosphere.

During reentry, the shuttle glides without using engines. It touches down on a runway using landing gear. A parachute then slows down the shuttle.

The *Magellan* spacecraft was launched from the cargo bay of the space shuttle *Atlantis*.

USA

Launching Satellites

Space shuttles take more than just astronauts into space. Shuttles also carry **satellites**, equipment, and other spacecraft in their **cargo bays**. Inside the cargo bay is a long robot arm. Astronauts use the robot arm to release satellites into space or catch them for return to Earth.

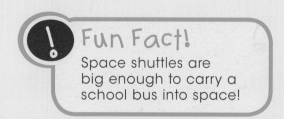

Fun Fact!
Space shuttles are big enough to carry a school bus into space!

The *Hubble Space Telescope*

Shuttles also carry **telescopes** and other equipment to help scientists. In 1990, the space shuttle *Atlantis* launched the *Hubble Space Telescope*. Astronomers use the telescope to study planets and stars.

Space shuttles are also used to fix the *Hubble Space Telescope*. The telescope rests in the shuttle's cargo bay while astronauts replace worn out parts.

Building a Space Station

Astronauts use space shuttles to build the *International Space Station*. Shuttles carry pieces of the station into space. Then astronauts put them together.

Astronauts use the shuttle's robot
arm to add parts to the station.
The robot arm holds the pieces as
astronauts bolt them in place.

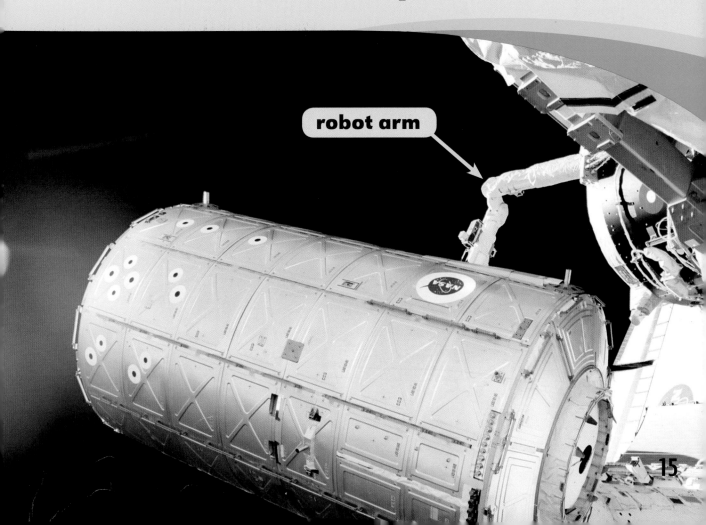

robot arm

Space Shuttle Accidents

Two space shuttles have been destroyed in accidents. On January 28, 1986, the shuttle *Challenger* exploded shortly after liftoff. All seven astronauts were killed.

On January 16, 2003, the shuttle *Columbia*'s wing was damaged during launch. The shuttle broke apart as it returned to Earth on February 1. All seven astronauts aboard the shuttle died.

A New Spacecraft

When the space station is completed, the space shuttles' job will be finished. A new, safer spacecraft named *Orion* will replace the shuttles. Astronauts will use *Orion* to reach the space station. They'll also use it to travel to the Moon.

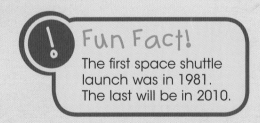

Fun Fact!
The first space shuttle launch was in 1981. The last will be in 2010.

Amazing but True!

Space shuttles always launch from Kennedy Space Center in Florida. But sometimes they have to land in California because of storms in Florida. When a shuttle lands in California, it gets back to Florida by catching a piggyback ride on top of a jet.

Think Big!

The external fuel tank played a role in both shuttle accidents. Flames leaking from a solid rocket booster caused *Challenger*'s external tank to explode. Pieces falling off the external tank caused the damage to *Columbia*'s wing. To make *Orion* safer, NASA is considering stacking the boosters, tank, and spacecraft on top of each other. Can you think of other ways to make *Orion* safe?

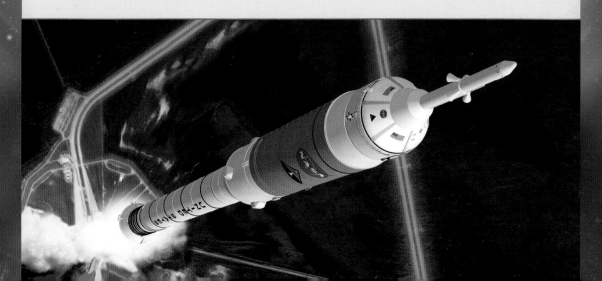

Glossary

atmosphere (AT-muhss-fihr) — the mixture of gases that surrounds Earth

booster (BOO-stur) — a rocket that gives extra power to a spacecraft

cargo bay (KAR-goh BAY) — area in a shuttle that carries equipment and satellites

external tank (ek-STUR-nuhl TANGK) — fuel container on the outside of a spacecraft

orbit (OR-bit) — to travel around an object in space; an orbit is also the path an object follows while circling an object in space.

satellite (SAT-uh-lite) — a spacecraft that circles Earth; satellites take pictures and send messages to Earth.

telescope (TEL-uh-skope) — a tool that makes faraway objects look larger and closer

Read More

Bredeson, Carmen. *Liftoff!* Rookie Read-About Science. New York: Children's Press, 2003.

Kerrod, Robin. *Space Shuttles.* The History of Space Exploration. Milwaukee: World Almanac Library, 2004.

Rees, Peter. *Secrets of the Space Shuttle.* Shockwave. New York: Children's Press, 2007.

Internet Sites

FactHound offers a safe, fun way to find Internet sites related to this book. All of the sites on FactHound have been researched by our staff.

Here's how:
1. Visit *www.facthound.com*
2. Choose your grade level.
3. Type in this book ID **1429612592** for age-appropriate sites. You may also browse subjects by clicking on letters, or by clicking on pictures and words.
4. Click on the **Fetch It** button.

Facthound will fetch the best sites for you!

Index